ALL AROUND THE WORLD
AUSTRIA

by Kristine Spanier, MLIS

Ideas for Parents and Teachers

Pogo Books let children practice reading informational text while introducing them to nonfiction features such as headings, labels, sidebars, maps, and diagrams, as well as a table of contents, glossary, and index.

Carefully leveled text with a strong photo match offers early fluent readers the support they need to succeed.

Before Reading

- "Walk" through the book and point out the various nonfiction features. Ask the student what purpose each feature serves.
- Look at the glossary together. Read and discuss the words.

Read the Book

- Have the child read the book independently.
- Invite him or her to list questions that arise from reading.

After Reading

- Discuss the child's questions. Talk about how he or she might find answers to those questions.
- Prompt the child to think more. Ask: Music is an important part of Austrian life. Do you play an instrument? Do you sing? Do you like listening to music?

Pogo Books are published by Jump!
5357 Penn Avenue South
Minneapolis, MN 55419
www.jumplibrary.com

Copyright © 2022 Jump!
International copyright reserved in all countries. No part of this book may be reproduced in any form without written permission from the publisher.

Library of Congress Cataloging-in-Publication Data

Names: Spanier, Kristine, author.
Title: Austria / by Kristine Spanier, MLIS.
Description: Minneapolis: Jump!, Inc., 2022.
Series: All around the world
Includes index. | Audience: Ages 7-10
Identifiers: LCCN 2020047912 (print)
LCCN 2020047913 (ebook)
ISBN 9781645279945 (hardcover)
ISBN 9781645279952 (paperback)
ISBN 9781645279969 (ebook)
Subjects: LCSH: Austria—Juvenile literature.
Classification: LCC DB17 .S584 2022 (print)
LCC DB17 (ebook) | DDC 943.6—dc23
LC record available at https://lccn.loc.gov/2020047912
LC ebook record available at https://lccn.loc.gov/2020047913

Editor: Jenna Gleisner
Designer: Molly Ballanger

Photo Credits: emperorcosar/Shutterstock, cover, 8-9; imageBROKER/Alamy, 1; Pixfiction/Shutterstock, 3; Tatiana Popova/Shutterstock, 4, 10; Yasonya/Shutterstock, 5; GanzTwins/iStock, 6-7; cristi180884/Shutterstock, 11; LordRunar/iStock, 12-13; TPG/Getty, 14; Epiximages/iStock, 15; Alamy, 16-17; algus/Shutterstock, 18-19; pressdigital/iStock, 20-21; RomanR/Shutterstock, 23.

Printed in the United States of America at Corporate Graphics in North Mankato, Minnesota.

TABLE OF CONTENTS

CHAPTER 1
Welcome to Austria!...................4

CHAPTER 2
A Royal History...................10

CHAPTER 3
Life in Austria...................14

QUICK FACTS & TOOLS
At a Glance...................22
Glossary...................23
Index...................24
To Learn More...................24

CHAPTER 1

WELCOME TO AUSTRIA!

Would you like to ski down a mountain? Maybe you would like to drink cocoa in Innsbruck. This city is nestled in the mountains.

Innsbruck

Or you could visit an **alpine** lake, like Lake Hallstatt. This is Austria! Summers here are warm enough to jump in the water. Welcome!

Lake Hallstatt

The Alps are a large mountain range. They cover more than half the country. Grossglockner is the tallest mountain. It reaches 12,461 feet (3,798 meters). People climb it. The trip can take two days!

WHAT DO YOU THINK?

Are there mountains where you live? If so, do you know what the tallest peak is? What other **landforms** do you live near?

CHAPTER 1 | 7

The Danube River flows in the north. It is the second longest river in Europe. It is 1,777 miles (2,860 kilometers) long. Many **ports** are along the Danube. A blue bell tower is in Dürnstein!

CHAPTER 1

CHAPTER 2
A ROYAL HISTORY

Royalty once ruled Austria. The Habsburg family ruled for nearly 650 years. You can still see their treasures in museums!

crown

They lived in the Schönbrunn Palace in the summers. You can now visit it. It has 1,441 rooms! **Emperor** Francis I opened a zoo here in 1752. Today, more than 700 different kinds of animals live here.

Schönbrunn Palace

The Habsburgs' rule ended after World War I (1914–1918). A president now leads the country. The Federal Assembly makes laws. It meets in the Hofburg Imperial Palace in Vienna. Vienna is the **capital**.

CHAPTER 3
LIFE IN AUSTRIA

Wolfgang Amadeus Mozart was born in Salzburg in 1756. He is considered one of the greatest music **composers** of all time. Music is still important in Austria. The Vienna Boys Choir started in 1498!

Children start school when they are six years old. They attend until they are 15. Then some prepare for college. Others start training for jobs.

Austrians are proud of their **heritage**. Some wear **traditional** clothing every day. Others save these outfits for special occasions.

TAKE A LOOK!

Traditional Austrian outfits are called trachten. What are the pieces called? Take a look!

CHAPTER 3   17

Would you like to try apple strudel? This dessert is a **national** dish. Chocolate cake is also popular.

WHAT DO YOU THINK?

What desserts and other foods are popular where you live? Why do you think they're popular? If you could choose a national dessert, what would it be? Why?

apple strudel

CHAPTER 3 · 19

December is a special time in Austria. People gather at Christmas markets. They shop for toys and gifts. Some go for horse carriage rides. Ice skating is fun, too! Would you like to visit?

DID YOU KNOW?

Krampus **festivals** take place during the Christmas season. Krampus is a figure from a **legend**. It was believed he punished naughty children. People dress in scary costumes.

QUICK FACTS & TOOLS

AT A GLANCE

AUSTRIA

Location: Central Europe

Size: 32,383 square miles (83,872 square kilometers)

Population: 8,859,449 (July 2020 estimate)

Capital: Vienna

Type of Government: federal parliamentary republic

Languages: German, Slovene, Croatian, Hungarian

Exports: machinery and equipment, vehicles and parts, iron and steel

Currency: euro

GLOSSARY

alpine: Of, relating to, or resembling the Alps.

capital: A city where government leaders meet.

composers: People who write or create things, such as pieces of music, stories, or poems.

emperor: The ruler of an empire.

festivals: Celebrations or holidays.

heritage: Traditions and beliefs that a country or society considers an important part of its history.

landforms: Natural features of land surfaces.

legend: A story handed down from earlier times. Legends are often based on fact, but they are not entirely true.

national: Of, having to do with, or shared by a whole nation.

ports: Towns or cities with harbors where ships can load and unload goods.

royalty: A king, queen, or member of his or her family.

traditional: Having to do with the customs, beliefs, or activities that are handed down from one generation to the next.

Austria's currency

INDEX

Alps 7
apple strudel 18
Christmas markets 21
Danube River 8
dessert 18
Dürnstein 8
Emperor Francis I 11
Europe 8
Federal Assembly 12
Grossglockner 7
Habsburg family 10, 12
Hofburg Imperial Palace 12
Innsbruck 4
Krampus 21
Lake Hallstatt 5
mountain 4, 7
Mozart, Wolfgang Amadeus 14
ports 8
Schönbrunn Palace 11
school 15
trachten 17
Vienna 12
Vienna Boys Choir 14
World War I 12

TO LEARN MORE

Finding more information is as easy as 1, 2, 3.
1. Go to www.factsurfer.com
2. Enter "Austria" into the search box.
3. Choose your book to see a list of websites.